Will You Marry ME?

Before I Do, Let Us Talk About...

Will You Marry ME?

Before I Do, Let Us Talk About...

Dr. Mary Lewallen

Thank you, God, for creating marriage.
I am so happy to have found love.
I will fulfill the role you have given me as a spouse

Today is a very special day; I get to share it with everyone; they are waiting at the dinner table for me. I'm surprised at the turnout on my special day. Everyone is here because of my birthday! This is such a surprise to me; I really feel loved. But where is he? I don't see him; maybe he was caught in traffic. Let me call and see what is going on with him. The phone rings: hey, are you not coming to my birthday party? Yea, but I am busy now. Talk to you later, I will be there. The phone hangs up without saying bye. Something is not right. Well, I am going to enjoy myself. Hello everyone, I am so happy you guys could come.

I sit down at the table and look around to see if he would walk through the door. My heart is sad, but my strong will refuses to show it. I want to cry badly, but I refuse to mess up this beautiful day. I ordered sweet tea and looked at the menu. I hear a voice that sounds familiar singing the Happy Birthday song. But when he got closer, he was saying, Will You Marry Me? He got on his knees in front of me. I was sweating, and tears were coming from my eyes. My body was shaking, and my knees were trembling. Then he opened this small box and there it was, the ring of my dreams. What should I say? How should I respond?

We have never talked about marriage. Where is this going? My mind is racing all over the place. Should I say No in front of all these people?

You may say NO!

Will You Marry ME?

Editors

Bishop Ken Lewallen

Prophetess Tashaye. K. Doss

Bible Credit

The version of the Scriptures is taken from the King James Version and used as a public domain. Unless otherwise showed, all Scripture references are taken from the King James Version (KJV) and New International Version (NIV)

Contents

Before I Do, Let Us Talk About...

Relationship Intervention for Oneness

Relationship Intervention Oneness (RIO) is a tool God gave me to help couples understand a healthy kingdom-minded relationship. This book brings the questions to the forefront that no one wants to talk about. Through communication, interaction, and emotions. Also, it is a guiding tool that can prevent severe relationship problems, engagement, marriage, or courtship. Each principle given is to assist, support, and aid. The Word of God is used in this book as an instrument that imparts Godly strategies to encamp your relationship.

What does RIO stand for?

- Relationship - A connection that establishes a covenant should not be broken by either person because it is a spiritual, emotional, and physical covenant.
- Intervention - Involve oneself in a situation to alter or hinder an action that is development or cause harm/damage to a relationship.
- Oneness- United in thoughts, emotions, and Spirit, soul, body, and mind. For example, the Bible defines marriage as two becoming one. (1+1 = 1).

Golden Nugget: a successful relationship is connected like a triangle God the Father, a man, a woman, the Word of God the foundation, and in the middle is the Holy Spirit.

Dedication

I take this time to thank God for His many blessings. I thank Him for allowing me this opportunity to write. I know that I could have not done this alone but with the leading of the Holy Spirit. Today and always, I will praise my God Jehovah! In all things will I give thanks! Thank you, Jesus!

~

I dedicated this book to my lovely family, friends, and my church family. Thank you to my husband, Bishop Ken Lewallen, and a special dedication to my three children, Tashaye, Shanitha, and Michael. These three have been a great help to me. I just want to say I love you, and with your help and understanding, this is possible. Thanks, guys, you rock!

A Message from the Author

If you are looking for a book that will give insight into building a healthy relationship and cut no corners, look no further. This is the book! This is a Christian self-help book written to communicate and explain to the readers the importance of saying, Will You Marry Me or "I do, or Do I?" This book is an investment in your marriage, relationship, engagement, and courtship.

There is no magic portion you can do to make a have a healthy Marriage Relationship. You must put the work into it and stay consistent. Marriage is not a fairy tale or a television picture for entertainment; it is actual life. This book focuses on the words most of us want to hear or have said, "Will You Marry Me?" These simple words are so significant in their meaning. When you say "I Do," It says, I am aware of his/her expectations of me, and in my role as the husband or wife, I will meet their expectations.

This book aids in explaining what is behind the words will you marry me and "I do." It provides mental and spiritual principles to help you understand what goes on behind the mental thoughts of "I do." Some character buildings must occur before and after you say, "I do," to avoid having second thoughts.

Think About It

Family

Do I Love This Person More Than...
My family ....
My children ....
My ex-spouse ....
My relationship with my ex- ....
My parents ....
Nurture when they are sick ....
Their family member to visit ....

Finance

Do I Love This Person More Than...
My money ....
My job ....
My bills ....
Their bills ....
No Job would I stay? ....
Putting our money in the same bank Account ....

Material Things

Do I Love This Person More Than...
Enough to let them drive my new car....................................
The house or apartment I live in ....
To move to their location ....
To lie for them..
Forgive the hurts that they cause ....

Relationship Prayer

Father, teach us your ways when dealing with each other. We place you as the head of our engagement and marriage. We are two different people willing to come together in unity to show our love. You brought us together, and we know that You have a plan and a purpose for us. If we obey Your Word, you will prosper us and not harm us.

Remind us you are the center of our relationship and that You are the one who watches over our future. We look to you for wisdom and guidance. May your peace surpasses all understanding and guard our hearts and minds through Jesus Christ our Lord, Amen.

Preface

You found the person you want to spend the rest of your life with through marriage. You are not the only person; so many like you are ready to say I do. Everyone looks forward to that day when they can join in Holy Matrimony with the person they love. Genesis 2:18 states, *"It is not good for the man to be alone. I will make a helper suitable for him."* You were made just the way God wanted you to be made. God made man for woman and woman for man. There is no doubt as to whom we were created for and whom we served.

Now you have that engagement ring, you are excited, and all your time now is spent on wedding preparation. You are focused on the hype of being engaged until you have overlooked some significant red flags. Before the music stops and the wedding's fresh flowers dry up, and everyone is gone home. Everyone has left the wedding and reception, and it is just you and your bride/groom. Think about what it takes to have a healthy engagement, relationship, and marriage. Do not wait until it is too late to talk about issues and concerns. Before any wedding preparations, let's talk about our relationship.

Many couples do not invite Jesus into their relationship, nor invite Him to their wedding ceremony or reception. He does not take part in where He was not invited. You never invite Him to come and dine, but you want Him to come and take care of them when faced with problems.

The Bible talks about when Jesus was invited to the wedding, and a great miracle was performed. When you invite Jesus, and He attends, and anointing comes and hovers in the atmosphere. Jesus will bless the marriage when He arrives.

In the book of John, the wedding has run out of wine. The Bible says Jesus turned water into wine, and that blessed the wedding. The bride and groom were blessed, but everyone who attended the wedding received a blessing as well. The fact that the miracle was performed at a wedding is also significant. As Christian, you should want to invite Jesus to our wedding. Often, we invite everyone we know to show off, including the devils, but never take the time to invite the cornerstone of the relationship, which is Jesus!

There is a difference between a believer's wedding and a non-believer; the difference is Jesus Christ is the center of the wedding. When you bring Jesus in, He will reside there, unite goals, give purpose, and inspire others to do the same.

Jesus will make sure that the marriage will grow in the image of God. Whereas non-Christians may focus on entertaining the guest for popularity. The Holy Spirit works in maturing each one so that the goal of Christlikeness becomes increasingly clear in the relationship. When you make Jesus the center of the relationship, the center of the union, the Holy Spirit leads each person to become more like the Creator instead of their own individual self. He brings their marriage into a unit of oneness.

Another critical component in a Christian marriage is selflessness; the Bible states that if you *Fulfil ye my joy, that ye be likeminded, having the same love, being of one accord, of one mind. Let nothing be done through strife or vainglory; but in lowliness of mind let each esteem other better than themselves. Look not every man on his own things, but every man also on the things of others. Let this mind be in you, which was also in Christ Jesus: (Philippians 2:2-4).* These marriage components are essential for both persons in the relationship. This should be done before you get married; you must be willing to walk together on one accord, with one mind, in the lowliness of your minds. To walk in humility is not to feel like your right all the time and to know that you are not right all the time.

Also, accepting others may be right as well, and their opinion matters. You should already walk in the strength of humility before you walk down the aisle.

With that said, the Bible states, *"Better it is to be of a humble spirit with the lowly than to divide the spoil with the proud."* *(Proverbs 16:19)* A house divide cannot stand when it comes to problems, troubles, and struggles.

"A man's pride shall bring him low: but honour shall uphold the humble in spirit." *(Proverbs 29:23)* You must practice maintaining your honor, working and managing humility daily in the relationship or marriage. Because your ideas and thoughts are subject to be wrong. Pride says you are right,

but honor says you are humble. When you establish that humbleness, it is vital to you, your relationship, and your marriage.

You should make every effort to ensure that you bent over backward and walk in humility. When in a marriage, you must consider his/her needs before your own needs. Through the power of the Holy Spirit, you can achieve this self-sacrificing task of humility. Jeremiah warns that if you do not humble yourself, principalities shall come down on you. *"Say unto the king and to the queen, Humble yourselves, sit down: for your principalities shall come down, even the crown of your glory."* (Jeremiah 13:18)

Also, one of the Holy Spirit's duties is to enable you to perfect the Spirit of Humility by guiding you daily with the Word of God. When you and your partner develop and practice humility, it will bring a strong union to your marriage.

Togetherness fortifies and strengthens your relationship and marriage. Pray before the engagement then, pray at the wedding ceremony and pray for the marriage.

It is time you think about the person you are going to marry. There is life after the wedding day and before the wedding day.

Call Jesus and Invite Him to Your Wedding

When a couple decides to get married, it is their responsibility to invite Jesus to the relationship, the wedding, and the marriage. One of the guests you want to make sure attends the wedding is Jesus Christ, Our Lord and Savior. In today's society, the presence of God and His Holy Throne is not invited to the wedding ceremony. Most weddings are focused more on worldly traditions than Godly focused. The whole wedding is about elevating your flesh. You give yourself an exempt ticket to indulge in the flesh. Then you focus on giving that day to the world, not God. When you start a relationship and give in to the devil, he will steal, kills, and destroys what you thought was yours.

As soon as you allow God into your union, He can handle every situation, every trouble, and every problem in the atmosphere. He brings Trinity's presence in the room and waits for them to bring forward a miracle. In fact, when Jesus is invited, He gives direction to those who are willing to obey. The Bible states that if two or three are gathered in His name, He is in the middle.

"For where two or three are gathered together in my name, there am I in the midst of them." (Matthew 18:20

This is a list of ways to invite Jesus into the Relationship, Wedding, and Marriage.

- Pray daily for guidance

- Pray together for obedience

- Deny yourself from the bed

- Deny yourself from fornication

- Deny yourself from any strong drink

- Pray for the direction of the relationship

- Pray Before the Wedding

- Acknowledging His Love for you and your partner

- Read the Word of God daily and practice what you read

- Singing Praises unto God

- Reverence Worship in His arena

- Pray after the Wedding

- Pray before the Reception

- Give Thanksgiving to the Highest God

Preparations

What I need to know about what I do?

When you say, "I do," problems come from out the woodworks! Remember, Jacob tricked his brother Esau to give up his birthright. Don't you get tricked by the devil! Keep your eyes open! When he wanted to get married, he was tricked as well. Jacob operated as a deceiver, a manipulator, and a conniver. But when it was time to take a wife, he seeks sound advice from his parents. Jacob knew his ideas would be tainted. For instance, in *Genesis 28:1-5,* Isaac gave his son Jacob some advice: do not marry a Canaanite woman because she does not know God or revere Him. Listen, oil and water don't mix.

His father gave him directions on where to go to find a wife. Most Christians marry people who do not revere their God. When you do that, expect tough battles in your relationship and marriage. It is a brutal battle when you are dealing with someone that does not love your God. What you do when you are single will raise you up when you get married. What you sow, you will reap! When Jacob married, he had many challenges. What Jacob did while he was single, showered in his life when he was married?

Jacob was deceived into marrying someone else; then, when he finally married the woman he wanted, she was barren. Jacob could live with this because he had prayed to God before he said, "I do." He knew that he had married someone who understood his anointing and the call on his life. I am giving you the advice to make sure you love someone that loves your God. It will be tough to bring your relationship or marriage in unity with God when your potential fiancée does not love the true and living God.

Often, when you are engaged, you will overlook shortcomings and tell yourselves love conquers all. You say he/she will change, and you ignored warning signs. Before you say, I do, make sure you have prayed and requested directions from the Lord. It is important to ask yourself this question: DO I?

Write all the things you dislike about your future spouse. For example, his/her annoying habits good or bad. For instance, I dealt with my finance licking his fingers while he ate. That would drive me crazy, but as we continue dating, I said how that bothers me. At first, he was puzzled why it annoyed me and felt that these were his fingers, not mine.

I enjoy my food this way. I said, but we are out, and people are looking at us. He said, okay, I will stop, but that took his happiness when he would eat. Make sure you will deal with the effect of what you are asking. I prayed about it, God gave me peace, and I love to see him enjoy his food when I cook.

It is your duty to acknowledge God and seek His guidance and direction before you say I do. If you seek and search for God before the marriage, you will have no problem finding Him in the Marriage. The scripture says, *"But seek ye first the kingdom of God, and his righteousness; and all these things shall be added unto you."* (Matthew 6:33)

You must allow God to guide your relationship and marriage; however, it is hard to let God come in when you do not even have a close relationship with Him. When you have not met Him personally, you cannot meet Him spiritually or take orders from Him when you do not know Him. You must say I do to God before saying I do to your future spouse.

Your relationship with God means more than your relationship with your future spouse. Because your relationship with God will affect the quality of your relationship with your future spouse. If you are looking to have a good relationship with your spouse, start with a good relationship with God.

One way to have a successful marriage is by fasting and praying. Each of you must have a personal relationship with God to clearly hear Him through fasting, praying, and worshiping. Also, find the correct place for people who are close to you or your future spouse.

For instance, parents, siblings, in-laws, children from previous marriage, cousins, and friends all have a place in your life. You will receive advice from all of them. My grandmother would always say the advice is like a fish, eating the meat, and tossing the bones. You can listen, and if it does not apply to your situation, toss the bones and eat the meat.

It is best for your relationship and future marriage to clearly decide how to handle family and friends commenting on your relationship. If you do not have a solid foundation, it will easily be broken by others. Remember, they are not trying to hurt you, just making sure you do not get hurt.

When you decide who to receive advice from, family or friends, determine if it will help or hinder. My advice is not to open up your engagement or marriage to everyone but to choose your circle wisely. Take the time to listen and hear what they have to say; if you feel they have your best interest at heart, then pray about their position in the course of the marriage and relationship.

Always pray about the advice someone gives you before you act on it. Ensure you have established mutual family and friends' boundaries that you both adhere to in the relationship. Once you have established healthy boundaries in your relationship, they will run over into your marriage. Then, each person will know their role, what is expected of them in their role, and what is unacceptable in your marriage.

Unhealthy Boundaries

Unhealthy boundaries can be dangerous to your relationship and marriage. They become toxins over a long period. Unestablished boundaries with family and friends will cause you to second-guess every decision you have made, even after praying. You do not need this type of influence in your relationship or your marriage. Some people can divide a house into separate domains.

They pry into every situation that has nothing to do with them. They impose and interrupt your life by voicing their opinion on your private matters. They will hog the spotlight, taking the attention off you and your partner because they have made it all about them. They will see or hear a minor mistake in your fiancée and will make a mountain out of it.

They will mention that mistake so much that it will make you think about your spouse's mistake or weakness. People will exaggerate one little weakness because it is unbearable to stand with them. Also, they can destroy a marriage, but not everyone who is a third party would have the heart to do that. God can use whoever He wants to get a message to you. Use discernment while listening to unsolicited advice.

Organize Your Marriage

Before you say, I do

The book of Ephesians gives insight into the organizational chart of marriage. First, there is Christ, the husband, and then the wife. *For the husband is the head of the wife, even as Christ is the head of the church: and he is the saviour of the body. (Ephesians 5:23)* In the book of Ephesians', *Wives, submit yourselves unto your own husbands, as unto the Lord. (Ephesians 5:22)* the husband is the leader of the body as Christ is the church body leader.

In the marriage organization chart, there is one person responsible for the entire organization, and it is that person who must answer to the board of directors. The heavenly host is the board of directors. Whereas the husband and wife are the managers. The entire organization does not have to answer the board. The president of the company speaks for everyone. With that said, it is the husband's responsibility to lead the family in the ways of the Lord. God will communicate to the husband when things are out of order, asking, where are thou? *The church is under Christ's authority, so wives are under their husbands' authority in everything.* (Ephesians 5:24)

The wife under the subject of her husband whereas, the husband is subject to God's authority in everything. When God came to the garden, He called Adam, not Eve. Because He had given the words of authority to Adam and it was

Adam's duty to inform His wife of her duties to the throne room.

Husbands, love your wives as Christ loved the church and gave his life for it. (Ephesians 5:25) There is a mandate for the husband to love their wives to the point of death. Let me explain the scripture it is impossible to love God and have no love for your wife. A husband must love the wife with a sacrificial love willing to give your life for her. Paul says that He did this to make the church holy and clean by washing and believing God's spoken Word. It is the husband's assignment to present his family to God daily. *He did this to make the church holy by cleansing it, washing it using water along with spoken words. (Ephesians 5:26) Then he could present it to himself as a glorious church, without any kind of stain or wrinkle-holy and without faults. (Ephesians 5:27)*

As the husband, you must love your wife as you do yourself. You are the protector of the body. It is your commission to love, take care of your wife. This act shows God and her that you love her.

Therefore, husbands must love their wives as they love their own bodies. A man who loves his wife loves himself. (Ephesians 5:28) *No one ever hated his own body. Instead, he feeds and takes care of it, as Christ takes care of the church. (Ephesians 5:29) Every husband must love his wife as he loves himself, and wives should respect their husbands. (Ephesians 5:33)* Wives should respect the husband's authority as the protector of the body. God expects the husband and the wife to submit themselves to one another in revere of God. Now that you understand the organization chart, you can establish who will lead in what situation.

Ephesian does not say that the marriage is a dictatorship, talked down to, humiliating, or superior authority. As the husband, you should not talk condescending or arrogant to your wife. You should be the example of Christ's love and leading of the church. Christ exhibits the following leadership skill set: compassion, mercy, forgiveness, respect, and selflessness. In the same manner and image, love your wife.

Ephesians says, "Submit to one another to worship Christ" Through the book of Ephesians, God is giving accountability to both the husband and the wife in the marriage. He is establishing authority for the structure of the home and the church. Three elements take place in a marriage, and they are vital factors.

Respect, submission, and *love* must be displayed in a marriage for it to survive the wiles of the devil. The husband and the wife must respect, love, and submit to their marriage at all times. To have a healthy marriage with Christ as the cornerstone, you must practice what you know is right. Understanding those principles and practicing them lead the husband and wife to produce a Christ-like image to develop and enhance your marriage.

When you exercise respect, love, and submission, your marriage will bloom like a flower over time. You must understand that the Bible gives your clear explanation of what is expected in a marriage.

Organize Your Marriage- P2

The book of Philippians 2:2-4 can be applied to a marriage. It states, that *Fulfil ye my joy, that ye be likeminded, having the same love, being of one accord, of one mind. You are expected to operate in an agreement Spirit of joy with the same admiration towards each other with one goal in mind.* In your marriage you cannot let anything be done out of strife or vainglory. As the husband and the wife, you must remove your discord, dissension, rivalry from your heart before you say the words I Do. *Let nothing be done through strife or vainglory; but in lowliness of mind let each esteem other better than themselves. (Philippians 2:3)*

Also, never remind each other of their failures, making them feel worthless and unproductive. Instead, you should operate in the Spirit of humbleness, meekness, and gentleness. It is your responsibility to honor and reverence each other better than you do for yourself. In your marriage, you should give good opinions of each other no matter what. You should see the good or bring the good to life. *Look not every man on his own things, but every man also on the things of others. (Philippians 2:4)* You must examine your life and not be self-centered or selfish. When you allow selfness to enter your life, it will steer you down the road of pride.

You must seek the presence of God to ignite the fighter in you that will not let you operate in the Spirit of Pride. Our Bible reads that you must *"Humble yourselves in the sight of the Lord, and he shall lift you up."* *(James 4:10)* When both persons humble themselves, it will create a healthy relationship and marriage. Always consider the other person's feelings; we are expected to consider others' needs before ourselves. To consider someone else needs before your needs require self-sacrifice, you must have rid yourself of selfishness. God does not expect you to do this on your own He has left the comforter to guide and give directions. To walk in humility and selflessness, you must be led by the Holy Spirit. When you allow the Holy Spirit to take control, He gives you elements of God's image. The scripture says the Word of God is *sharper than any two-edged sword and cuts as deep as the place where soul and Spirit meet, the place where joints and marrow meet. God's Word judges a person's thoughts and intentions.* *(Hebrews 4:12)* A good marriage is built on spiritual disciplines—Praying, Fasting, Worshipping, Praising, and studying the Holy Scriptures.

I Do, Means to Fix Something

In the book of I Samuel 25:3 -27, David had sent his men to ask Nabal to send food to help him and his soldiers. Nabal was a rude man that operated in doing evil. The scripture says, Now the name of the man was Nabal, and the name of his wife Abigail: and she was a woman of good understanding, and of a beautiful countenance: but the man was churlish and evil in his doings, and he was of the house of Caleb. (1 Samuel 25:3)

Nabal had married a woman of thoughtfulness and beauty. You mustn't allow your beauty to outweigh your brains. Abigail was a woman that understood the type of man she had married. Besides, she was always fixing what he had messed up. He was greedy, mean Spirit, and had no hospitality. David heard Nabal had to shear his sheep and sent out ten young men to go to Nabal and greet him in his name: Then say to him, "Peace be both to thee, and peace be to thine house, and peace be unto all that thou hast." He said that your men were with us, and we did not let them get hurt, nor did you lose anything. David told his servant to make sure they ask Nabal men if he did not believe them.

And David heard in the wilderness that Nabal did shear his sheep. (1 Samuel 25:4)

And David sent out ten young men, and David said unto the young men, Get you up to Carmel, and go to Nabal, and greet him in my name: (1 Samuel 25:5)

And thus shall ye say to him that liveth in prosperity, peace be both to thee, and peace be to thine house, and peace be unto all that thou hast. (1 Samuel 25:6)

Ask thy young men, and they will shew thee. Wherefore let the young men find favour in thine eyes: for we come in a good day: give, I pray thee, whatsoever cometh to thine hand unto thy servants, and to thy son David. (1 Samuel 25:8)

And when David's young men came, they spake to Nabal according to all those words in the name of David, and ceased. (1 Samuel 25:9)

And Nabal answered David's servants, and said, Who is David? and who is the son of Jesse? there be many servants now a days that break away every man from his master. (1 Samuel 25:10)

Shall I then take my bread, and my water, and my flesh that I have killed for my shearers, and give it unto men, whom I know not whence they be? (1 Samuel 25:11)

So David's young men turned their way, and went again, and came and told him all those sayings. (1 Samuel 25:12)

And David said unto his men, Gird ye on every man his sword. And they girded on every man his sword; and David also girded on his sword: and there went up after David about four hundred men; and two hundred abode by the stuff. (1 Samuel 25:13)

But one of the young men told Abigail, Nabal's wife, saying, Behold, David sent messengers out of the wilderness to salute our master; and he railed on them. (1 Samuel 25:14)

But the men were very good unto us, and we were not hurt, neither missed we any thing, as long as we were conversant with them, when we were in the fields: (1 Samuel 25:15)

They were a wall unto us both by night and day, all the while we were with them keeping the sheep. (1 Samuel 25:16)

Now therefore know and consider what thou wilt do; for evil is determined against our master, and against all his household: for he is such a son of Belial, that a man cannot speak to him. (1 Samuel 25:17)

Then Abigail made haste, took two hundred loaves, and two bottles of wine, and five sheep ready dressed, and five measures of parched corn, and an hundred clusters of raisins, and two hundred cakes of figs, and laid them on asses. (1 Samuel 25:18)

And she said unto her servants, Go on before me; behold, I come after you. But she told not her husband Nabal. (1 Samuel 25:19)

And it was so, as she rode on the ass, that she came down by the covert of the hill, and, behold, David and his men came down against her; and she met them. (1 Samuel 25:20)

Now David had said, Surely in vain have I kept all that this fellow hath in the wilderness, so that nothing was missed of all that pertained unto him: and he hath requited me evil for good. (1 Samuel 25:21)

So and more also do God unto the enemies of David, if I leave of all that pertain to him by the morning light any that pisseth against the wall. (1 Samuel 25:22)

And when Abigail saw David, she hasted, and lighted off the ass, and fell before David on her face, and bowed herself to the ground, (1 Samuel 25:23)

And fell at his feet, and said, Upon me, my Lord, upon me let this iniquity be: and let thine handmaid, I pray thee, speak in thine audience, and hear the words of thine handmaid.
(1 Samuel 25:24)

Let not my Lord, I pray thee, regard this man of Belial, even Nabal: for as his name is, so is he; Nabal is his name, and folly is with him: but I thine handmaid saw not the young men of my Lord, whom thou didst send. (1 Samuel 25:25)

Now therefore, my Lord, as the LORD liveth, and as thy soul liveth, seeing the LORD hath withholden thee from coming to shed blood, and from avenging thyself with thine own hand, now let thine enemies, and they that seek evil to my Lord, be as Nabal. (1 Samuel 25:26)

And now this blessing which thine handmaid hath brought unto my Lord, let it even be given unto the young men that follow my Lord. (1 Samuel 25:27)

I pray thee, forgive the trespass of thine handmaid: for the LORD will certainly make my Lord a sure house; because my Lord fighteth the battles of the LORD, and evil hath not been found in thee all thy days. (1 Samuel 25:28)

Yet a man is risen to pursue thee, and to seek thy soul: but the soul of my Lord shall be bound in the bundle of life with the LORD thy God; and the souls of thine enemies, them shall he sling out, as out of the middle of a sling. (1 Samuel 25:29)

And it shall come to pass, when the LORD shall have done to my Lord according to all the good that he hath spoken concerning thee, and shall have appointed thee ruler over Israel; (1 Samuel 25:30)

That this shall be no grief unto thee, nor offence of heart unto my Lord, either that thou hast shed blood causeless, or that my Lord hath avenged himself: but when the LORD shall have dealt well with my Lord, then remember thine handmaid. (1 Samuel 25:31)

And David said to Abigail, Blessed be the LORD God of Israel, which sent thee this day to meet me: (1 Samuel 25:32)

And blessed be thy advice, and blessed be thou, which hast kept me this day from coming to shed blood, and from avenging myself with mine own hand. (1 Samuel 25:33)

For in very deed, as the LORD God of Israel liveth, which hath kept me back from hurting thee, except thou hadst hasted and come to meet me, surely there had not been left unto Nabal by the morning light any that pisseth against the wall. (1 Samuel 25:34)

So David received of her hand that which she had brought him, and said unto her, Go up in peace to thine house; see, I have hearkened to thy voice, and have accepted thy person. (1 Samuel 25:35)

And Abigail came to Nabal; and, behold, he held a feast in his house, like the feast of a king; and Nabal's heart was merry within him, for he was very drunken: wherefore she told him nothing, less or more, until the morning light. (1 Samuel 25:36)

But it came to pass in the morning, when the wine was gone out of Nabal, and his wife had told him these things, that his heart died within him, and he became as a stone. (1 Samuel 25:37)

And it came to pass about ten days after, that the LORD smote Nabal, that he died. (1 Samuel 25:38)

And when David heard that Nabal was dead, he said, Blessed be the LORD, that hath pleaded the cause of my reproach from the hand of Nabal, and hath kept his servant from evil: for the LORD hath returned the wickedness of Nabal upon his own head. And David sent and communed with Abigail, to take her to him to wife. (1 Samuel 25:39)

And when the servants of David were come to Abigail to Carmel, they spake unto her, saying, David sent us unto thee, to take thee to him to wife. (1 Samuel 25:40)

And she arose, and bowed herself on her face to the earth, and said, Behold, let thine handmaid be a servant to wash the feet of the servants of my Lord. (1 Samuel 25:41)

And Abigail hasted, and arose, and rode upon an ass, with five damsels of hers that went after her; and she went after the messengers of David, and became his wife. (1 Samuel 25:42)

David also took Ahinoam of Jezreel; and they were also both of them his wives. (1 Samuel 25:43)

But Saul had given Michal his daughter, David's wife, to Phalti the son of Laish, which was of Gallim. (1 Samuel 25:44)

Do people tell you, you have a mean Spirit or you are rude for no reason? Do your fiancée feels you talk down to him or her and that you are stingy? You must fix those problems before you say I do. Ask yourself some hard truths. Look at all the relationships in your life. What name would they say you are? Are you always on the receiving end? How much of your time, support, and resources do you give back to the people who have invested in you?

Are you always looking for someone to listen to your problem and pray for you, someone to help you with an assignment or responsibility, or support you with a financial need? Do you give as much as you receive from people back to people? Are you always looking out for yourself? Are you always complaining about everything and everyone? Do you find it hard to forgive; do you remember and still hold on to things people did 3, 5, 10, 15 years ago to hurt you?

Do you usually believe your own understanding of an issue or your opinion or suggestion is more meaningful and carries more weight than others? Are your prayer requests all about you? To fix the problems in your life, you must do a self-evaluation. Clean up the sled before you invite someone else to ride on there with you. Those minor problems will come as major roadblocks in your life.

Fix all Problems that could Hinder your I Do's

Ask God to forgive you of all your sins knowingly and unknowingly. Then ask God to release the Spirit of discernment in your life so that you will discern what the Holy Spirit is leading you to do. Discernment will equip you with the tools necessary to serve the Lord faithfully. When placing people in a circle of trust in your life, you must be led by the Holy Spirit.

You need discernment to help you process which is helpful to your relationship or harmful. Remember, you cannot go through marriage not communicating with your spouse or other people. You must fix yourself, not your fiancée. Discernment will tell you when to talk and when to stay quiet. Never open your mouth to speak and bring negative energy into the room about your marriage. Pray daily for discernment and walk by faith.

You need the understanding of how important it is to have a personal relationship with God. To overcome all forms of impurities and infirmity, say this simple prayer and believe in faith that it is done. If you do not know God, you must fix that as well.

This is a Sinner's Prayer:

Heavenly Father, I have sinned against You, broken Your laws. Today I ask Your forgiveness. I repent right now for every sin that I committed knowingly and unknowingly in the name of Jesus! I believe in faith that You have forgiven me, and Jesus is sitting on your right side making intercession for me. I know Jesus died for my sins and gave me a chance to live a saved and sanctified life. Father, I want to have a good marriage that is the model of the church's love through Jesus Christ, our Savior.

You must begin to work on the things that need to be fixed. In a marriage, your emotions and your personality must remain consistent. Your mood swings can destroy your relationship and marriage. You cannot be hot today in a relationship, cold tomorrow, low the next day, and expect to keep a positive communication and healthy relationship. YOU need to fix that before you commit to a lifelong relationship.

Come to an agreement with yourself first and understand what is expected of you. If you cannot understand what is happening to your personality, seek help from a mentor and trust person. Bring God into an intimate walk with you and allow the Holy Spirit to guide you daily.

It is your responsibility to fix things that are of concern before you say I do. Pray, Father, I ask in the name of Jesus Christ our Lord, Help me conquer my emotions and get them under control.

You know my heart, for You created me in Your image and likeness. Your heart is consistent with, and therefore, I want my heart to consist as well. Please do not let me ignore my problems, but I come to you to help me fix them. Also, because my emotions are changing, it makes my heart change as well. Lord, help me not to foolishly give my hands and heart to a person who will pull me in the wrong direction. Grant me the discernment to see beyond the surface and know Your will.

Father, destroy all selfishness, destroy these mood swings, destroy wavering, destroy anger, and destroy jealousies in my life and fill me with the genuine love of Christ. Then I can be a selfless spouse in my marriage relationship.

Unequally Yoke

Be ye not unequally yoked together with unbelievers: for what fellowship hath righteousness with unrighteousness? and what communion hath light with darkness? (2 Corinthians 6:14) And what concord hath Christ with Belial? or what part hath he that believeth with an infidel? (2 Corinthians 6:15)

The union of marriage and the fullness of its growth have a particular element that needs to be relevant in the marriage before I Do. That element is to be yoked together; to have a productive relationship or marriage, you must be yoked together. I believe yoke is two people walking and working together, pulling and carrying the marriage load. As they go in the same direction at all, times walking out their relationship or marriage to its full potential. When the relationship or marriage is unequally yoked, there is a chance of separation, and the strand of one person pulls while the other bucks against you. For example, if you have two people walking in the same direction, the destination is achieved at the highest level. When one person is going the other way, it is hard to pull and plow at the same time. You find it is difficult to keep hauling the relationship or marriage to the destination of happiness.

Not only is plowing hard but also plant, cultivate, digging. All will become problematic for the relationship and marriage. End results you will have a marriage with holes, craters, and gaps, causing the marriage to stand still and not move forward at all. Remember, when you have one person going the other way and the other person going the opposite way, your marriage is unequally yoked. To have a marriage in harmony as a believer, you must bring Christ into the relationship before bringing the worldviews. A marriage that is unequally yoke has its trials and test. For instance, do I keep my devotional life; do I continue to pay my tithes or continue attending church and supporting the cause? These issues must be addressed before I Do to establish a strong foundation in your relationship. Do you want to give up your beliefs for unfulfilling marriage that might not last?

Usually, when the believer in the marriage puts a foothold on to their Christian lifestyle and refuses to break, the non-believing spouse will have to be ostracized, disregard, laid on the sideline. Suppose they cannot understand the point of Bible study and prayer, missions' trips, or hospitality. In that case, they cannot or will not take part alongside the believing spouse in those activities.

The profound unity and oneness cannot flourish when one partner cannot fully participate in the other person's most important commitments.

The marriage experiences stress and break up; or it experiences stress and stays together, achieving some kind of truce that involves one spouse or the other capitulating in some areas, which leaves both parties feeling lonely and unhappy. Does this sound like the kind of marriage you want?

One that strangles your growth in Christ or strangles your growth as a couple, or does both? Think back to that oft-cited passage in 2 Corinthians 6:14 about being "unequally yoked." Most of us no longer live in a farming culture but try to visualize what would happen if a farmer yoked together, say, an ox and a donkey. The heavy wooden yoke, designed to harness the team's strength, would be uneven, as the animals are of different heights, weights, walk at different speeds and with different pace. Instead of harnessing the team's power to complete the task, the yoke would rub and chafe BOTH animals since the load would be distributed unequally. An unequal marriage is not just unwise for the Christian; it is also unfair to the non-Christian and will be a trial for them both. There are several ways an unequal relationship or marriage will have its challenges.

Family

- Can I love someone that does not honor their parents?
- How did I fall in love with a know-it-all person and attempts to take charge of everything in the relationship and marriage?
- How can I love someone that abuses my children?
- How did I fall in love with someone with no control over their money and put undue expectations on the marriage?
- How did I fall in love with someone that has no clue how to raise a child?
- How did I fall in love with someone that has not talked to his or her parents in years?
- How did I fall in love with someone that will not stop flirting?
- How did I fall in love with someone that incapable of loving me back?
- How did I fall in love with someone that walks in pride, arrogance, and selfishness?
- How did I fall in love with someone that steals from me?
- How did I fall in love with someone that committed a crime?

Before I Do, Let Us Talk About...

Before I Do

Before you say I do, you must get a full understanding of what is expected of you. Besides, what will you gain from your "I do"? Similarly, take time to learn who you are and what you like or dislike yourself. Next, begin writing self-evaluations of who you are; do not leave no stone unturned. To give yourself to someone else, you must have established who you are. Again, write what you think you need to improve on and stick to them.

To have a successful marriage relationship, you must learn and understand all the successful marriage principles. With that said, not every marriage relationship is the same.

What you require in your relationship, someone else might not require those standards. Keep this in mind every person is different, and their outlook on life is different as well. When you say I do, it is like going on a vacation; you prepare, fix any problem, and work out situations as you go. Because you are expecting to have a great vacation.

Examine the box below and compare the information.

Vacation Compared to Marriage

Vacation	Marriage
Preparation before going	Preparation before I do
You saving money for the trip	Begin saving money
Pick the best time	Pick the best time
Discuss where you want to go	Discuss where are you going
Meet with everyone that is going to get exact directions	Meet to get exact directions on what you will and won't do.
Research needs to be done when going on vacation, first the internet, asking close friends, or sending away additional information.	Three types of research you should do before saying I do. Test yourself, find out who you are, talk to a person you trust, and read the Bible about marriage.

In short, vacation does not just happen; they are planned, and marriage does not just happen; it is planned as well. Jeremiah 29:11 says, *"For I know the plans I have for you..."* When a vacation is planned, organized, and discussed with all partners, you will accomplish excellent results.

Also, the Bible says to write the vision and make it straightforward. When you decide where you want to go on vacation, you research?

You can research the internet, ask close friends, and send away for information. Often, we do more research for a vacation than we do for a marriage.

God gave me a vision of this diagram to put in the books I write about marriage. This triangle has three sides and three levels on each side. The foundation of the triangle is founded on God's Word, which is Jesus; on the left side of the triangle is the woman and on the right is the man. In the middle, the Holy Spirit moving and working on your behalf. God is on top as He first in the marriage.

This is the **Marriage Covenant Triangle:** Apostle Paul explains in 2 Timothy 3:16 how the Word of God blesses our lives if we allow it. It brings inspiration; it rebukes when necessary for correction, for instruction in righteousness:

Before I Do, Let Us Talk About – Communicate

Communication is a vital element of a relationship and a marriage, whether it is verbal or nonverbal. I believe that communication has three compartments in a marriage. Leading by the Holy Spirit, He spoke to me and said that communication has three elements: expressing, listening, and signaling. These elements must be active when communicating. For instance, when you are talking to someone, and he/she is not listening, you can tell because they cannot answer any question you ask. Also, there is a signal that you see to let you know they are not listening. When you see that, you immediately shut down and refuse to keep talking. Often when this happens, your relationship is on its way down the broken highway of communication, and your marriage is on its way to a divided house.

Another point, when communication stops, whether verbal or non-verbal, emotions stop as well. When people don't express their thoughts or ideas, they feel less valued. When someone's feelings and opinions are unnecessary, then his or her self-worth replenishes. For example, teenagers will stop talking to you if they feel you don't value their thoughts, ideas, or emotions.

Take into consideration you are not in a relationship with a mind reader. Think of this: you cannot correct communication problems if you do not know there are problems. Therefore, talk about it, actively listen and show the sign of understanding Express, listen and signal by talking as if you did when you were dating, not at each other, not critically. Just talk.

Before I Do, Let Us Talk About - child (ren) Born or Unborn

Do you want children? How many? Will you work? How will we discipline our children? You cannot think you will be the better parent when there are no children. When the children come, it is all a different story. Don't forget you and your spouse are on the same team; not you and your child are on the same team against Mom or against Dad. If you disagree with your spouse on how to parent, talk it out later and understand what is best for the household. It is important to handle these matters before bringing a wedge between your relationships if you allow it. When there is an opening in the relationship concerning children, the other spouse feels disrespected and unloved, leading to disastrous results, especially if it becomes routine behavior.

As for the unborn, decide on how many and how soon. This should be done by you and your partner; no one else should have a say so. Also, talk about the name of the children to avoid any heartfelt feelings.

Before I Do, Let Us Talk about - Step-Children

Often a person has a child or two from a previous relationship. This can become a problem in your marriage if you do not establish what is acceptable and unacceptable. You cannot blame the children for your failed marriage; only blame yourself! Children can make you jealous of their relationship with their parents. It is okay to allow the parent to spend alone time with their child (ren). This must be established at the beginning of the relationship.

Second, children will make you feel insecure about the marriage by bringing up what their parents did before you. They seem to always invite the ex around, which makes you uncomfortable to the point that you begin to sabotage your only relationship by staying at home and not going.

Third, the child's support must be paid. You must understand that this is not negotiable; good parents take pride in taking care of their children. If you are with someone not taking care of their children, they will not take care of yours. That's a fact, Jack! You must talk about finances to make sure you can have a comfortable life that includes your children.

When you both have children allow them to meet each other. Don't force them to befriend; just let it happen. With adult children, discussion of how things and situations will be handled with them must be made. If they make poor choices when it comes to money, there must be an agreement on the limit. Lastly, when you bring your children, and they bring their children, you will get different views from each child's perspective. You must establish dos and don'ts and give the penalty when the rules are broken. I know that you cannot change the rules once established without letting all partners know of the change and have agreed. Remember, if you were the reason parents left their spouse, it is hard for children to understand when they are taught not to give up, but you did. On the other hand, if you feel guilty for your marriage's failure and cannot understand how to make things work with your children, pray and seek counseling.

Before I Do, Let Us Talk About - Immaturity

Immaturity is when an adult has lived a life with no responsibilities and no consequences for their actions. They tend to not behave in a way that is expected of a person of their age. There are three immature levels: the babyish stage, the childish stage, and the juvenile stage. These levels affect males and females.

The babyish stage is when the person wants you to do everything for them. Feed them, clean up after them, and work to take care of them. When it is their time to return the favor, they whine and complain about how unhappy they are.

With that said, the childish stage is when the adult behaves like that of a child. You can identify their behavior with that of a child. When it's time to be serious, they act silly; when everyone is having fun, they are not interested and spoil it for anyone else. Because they are unhappy. Lastly, when it's time to face reality in what they have done, they take no ownership of anything.

Last, the juvenile stage is when the adult acts, shows the character of a young person. They have severe mood swings that are unpredictable when you try to communicate with them. They dislike being around people; they are silent and love isolation.

They are always saying what they don't like and what they will not tolerate. But when it comes to stepping up to the plate and take responsibility, that is absent. In the Juvenile stage, they rather hang out with friends instead take responsibility as an adult. Another example of a juvenile adult is petty insults and a lack of tact. They say the wrong thing at the wrong time. If you share heartfelt secrets when they are in the rage, they will use that against you. And it does not matter who is standing around. You must sit, watch and notice if any of these signs you see in the person you just said I Do or going to say I Do.

When a person is immature in a relationship, there are many hurls you will have to jump or climb. You will fight over small things that this person should already know that are crucial to a relationship. But sometimes they really don't know, and no one has required them to stand up and or grow up. Sometimes they can try to overcome these stages with help and prayer. Again, you are on the same team. When you argue, ask yourself if what you're fighting for is worth possibly damaging your relationship or marriage.

Before I Do, - Let Us Talk About - Finance

You must get on the same financial page. Decide if you will have separate banks or share one bank account. When you decide to have a separate bank account, someone must have something to hide, or the lack of trust has made it arrive in your heart. Be open about your feelings regarding their spending or frugality.

The question is do I love you enough to trust you with my money or give you complete access to my money. How can you love a person but can't trust them with all of you? Before I do, sit down and create a budget with both persons available, and each of you brings your check stubs to the table and your bills to see the best option to become debt-free. Four financial situations can end a relationship and a marriage, hiding money, hiding debt, overspending, and under-spending.

Hiding money may seem like a good idea for your just in case moment. You might feel that it is not hurting anyone, or no suffering is taking place. In reality, it is lying, cheating, and stealing, with a heart that is deceitful and distrusting, and disloyal to the relationship and the marriage.

There is nothing in a marriage that can hide; it will surely come to light. Then that will be the downfall of your relationship or marriage.

To avoid hiding money, sit down with your significant other and let them know you have saved some money and why you have saved it. There should be a reason that you would go to this length to destroy your relationship or marriage. If you must hide money, give your partner the same opportunity or just get separate accounts.

Hiding debt is a great relationship killer. When you hide your debt, you are lying, cheating, and presenting a falsehood of your partner's money. When your partner thinks you guys are about to get out of debt and have a $10,000 bill, you did not add to the budget. You have acted a lie, implied a lie, and lived a lie. This type of distrust will bring many arguments that you brought on your own. There is no need to be deceitful in a marriage. If God sees you as one, why do you feel your money is two? You must recognize when you have fallen in love with your money. Solve this problem by sitting down and make sure you are on the same road of debt-free. Money is one of the most argued over subjects. It has destroyed families, marriages, and relationships. The Bible says the love of money is the root of all evil.

There should be a set amount of how much each of you will spend. Do not hide your debt; be honest and open about the debt you have.

Underspending is a different issue because it falls under the category of stingy. In a relationship and marriage, a person who is too tight with the money will cause problems. For example, you both have good jobs, but you insist on driving an old beat-up vehicle. You think it is saving money, and you have put more money in the vehicle each year. Your conversation is we can't afford it. Your vehicle is continually breaking down, and other people have to give you and your family rides. That becomes an embarrassment for the family. Solve this by sitting down, weighing all options and get the best buck for the money.

Last is overspending, which is when one of you makes more money than the other, and you feel it's my money, I can spend it as I please. This problem can quickly become financial abuse. You spend the money on yourself only. You buy yourself nice shoes and clothes. To solve this problem, agree to an allowance for both of you and stick to it. Do not love money more than you love your relationship and marriage. You will never find happiness in money and possessions.

How do you recognize when you love money?

1. You lie about it.

2. You hide it.

3. You steal it.

4. You divide it between yourself and your love.

5. You become disloyal to your marriage.

6. You say you are saving it, but you spend it for yourself.

7. You won't decide if it includes your money.

If you have answered yes to any of these, then you probably

love money

Nugget: Don't hide or steal money from your spouse.

Before I Do, Let Us Talk About - Dating Each Other

Often when a couple gets married, there is very little time for dating. When you were dating, both people would get dressed and eat at a quiet place and enjoy each other's company. That must still live in your marriage; sit down and decide how many date nights you can afford to have together.

Listen, do not forget to tell your wife or husband I miss you, you are so beautiful to me, women, tell your husband how handsome he looks to you. Always say things like you are the best woman or man I have ever cared for, and I love you dearly. Date your husband or wife while you are married to not stop dating. That's how you won each other over, and that's how you keep each other wanting to come home to you.

Another example of dating is when you cook, clean and run the bathwater. Get your candle salt bath smell goods and let your spouse relax without you. Let them immerse in the water and play some soft CHRISTIAN music.

Before I Do, Let Us Talk About - Extended Families

I love my family, and I know my husband loves his, but we know that our best supporter is each other. You must discuss healthy boundaries for your families. You must let your family know who is number one in your life. You should let them know that my spouse is my number one when I get married. Any decisions you make, you do them together and not with your father, mother, sister, or brother. You must respect your spouse in front of your family, and they will automatically do the same things.

Once you disrespect your spouse, the entire family will feel they may do the same things. Please never compare your family against their family. When you do that, it brings separation between the families. God creates every person differently, and therefore, we all have a uniqueness about us. Embrace that uniqueness; don't decay it.

Before I Do, Let Us Talk About - The Ex's

You cannot have a successful marriage when you are still addicted to your Ex. There are three areas marriage brings together that are body, mind, and soul. Men, women will respect you when you make her feel that she is the only woman you care about besides your mother. If you still have an attachment to your Ex, it cripples her love for you. Often you will be disrespected when the Ex comes around because she feels unsecured, unprotected, and unappreciated. Remember that you love this person, and your relationship with your Ex must have healthy boundaries. No sneaking in the corner, talking or going over to fix or repair something that is broken. You must respect your marriage and love the person you are marrying. This type of environment will destroy a relationship and marriage quickly. When you treat your Ex as if you are still together, it seems to your partner that you still have feelings for them. There should be a different way to how you treat your Ex compared to treat your new spouse. Calling your Ex daily is not a good idea when you have moved on with another relationship. In some cases, you cannot continue a friendship with your Ex once you marry.

Also, do not discuss your new relationship with your Ex. It is none of their business. You must sit down and establish some guidelines when it comes to Ex.

Before I Do, Let Us Talk About - Infertility

What are you willing to do if you can't have children and your spouse want them badly? Know your options and discuss them before you get married. There are many options out there, so don't give up. Research each option and see which one is best for you guys. Are you okay with adoption? How about a sperm donor? Remember there are lots of children that need parents. Have an open mind; do not ignore your spouse's feelings sabotage the process. You should both get checked by the doctor before you get married. If anything happens, it is not like you hid it.

Trying to start a family can be very stressful. You are on a team, and each player will need to understand how to win the games. There are so many worries that will travel through your mind. For instance, will I get married if he/she knows I can't have children? Try not to blame the other person or pass judgment on them. You should be more understand and come together to figure out how to overcome this obstacle. There may be a financial strain on the finance with the decision you both agree on at a particular time.

Before I Do, Let Us Talk About - Chores

Couples actually fight over who turns it is to do the dishes. When they have a dishwasher and wash their clothes. When one spouse feels he/she is working and doing all the housework, it becomes significant in the marriage? The stress level increases, and it is hard to live in peace. Their emotions will keep them unhappy, and they will eventually stop cleaning up altogether. This is definitely an issue that needs to be discussed before I do. They need to discuss their frustrations when they are calm and not when they are hot with arguments. You understand that house chores are no longer just for one person; it is a team effort. This issue is easy to solve, talk about it, and understand why, what, when, and how. Discuss every chore that needs to be done. Pick a day that you will complete your chores and stick to it. Once the chore is complete, do not criticize how the other person completes the chores. If you criticize, you will be left completing it yourself.

Before I Do, Let Us Talk About–Secrets

Secrets can handicap a marriage and relationship. You have the right to your own privacy, but some secrets must be told when you decide to get married or a serious relationship. If you do not tell, someone else will, and that is most hurtful. Here is a list of secrets that need your attention.

- Job Problem.
- Angry problem.
- Legal problem.
- Child support.
- Debt and Owing money.
- Addiction or substance abuse.
- Habits.
- Not paying bills.
- Bad Credit
- Not talking about various sick you have.
- Secretly visiting old friends and family of your Ex.
- Had an affair.
- Molestation.
- Rape.
- Adoption.

It is important to remember that you do not have to share everything with another person in a relationship. Also, it depends on how much you trust that person. Because you have the right to, as stated, your own privacy. No one tells secrets to be judged, criticized, put down, or talked about. Secrets are told out of honesty, trustworthiness, and open heartiness. Not to be scolded, called various names, or looked at differently.

Once a person tells you that something happens to them, do not bring it up again without permission. You cannot call your family and say you guys were right! Secrets must be kept between the two of you. Make sure you use common sense for some secrets.

If you want a healthy relationship and marriage, you will honor your vows and your words. You must take and stand and hold your mouth for secrets. When you tell a secret after it has been told to you. You notice intimacy is not the same; also, there is a void of emptiness in your relationship.

Maybe you have a secret that you want to share, but you do not know if you should. Tell it to yourself and see your response. Take yourself out of the equation and see how you would react to your secret. If your response is negative, hurtful, emotional fit. I think you should share that secret when the time is right.

This is different if you keep a secret because you don't want to face responsiveness or accountability, then that's a problem.

If you hold back on information that you know is true and your partner needs this information to decide, you manipulate your spouse for your benefit.

Before I Do, Let Us Talk About - What is on Your Mind?

Often couples forget to express what is on their mind. A woman will vamp to her friend, but not to her partner and vice versa for a man. When you get to this point, you must discuss what is on your mind. Even if you think they will not understand. It is very important to keep the communication line open when you are in a relationship. Be willing to express those deep thoughts. People are afraid to express themselves because one time or another, they did, and it backfired in their faces. Out of that were name-calling, hurtful words, and broken trust. When you decide to talk about what is on your mind, make sure it is safe. Authentic communication is telling the truth about how you feel and what is bothering you. Release what is on your mind daily. Pick a time to make sure your spouse is in the mood to listen. Do not get offended if they tell you not right now. Respect that and ask what will be a better time.

Before I Do, Let Us Talk About - Why do you want to Marry Me?

This should not be hard to answer at all. When you get to this point, it is okay to ask why? Often, we don't ask why you want to marry me and for how long. You can ask what if you said the change, will you still want to marry me? Most people will answer that question with hesitation. Because they have not thought of why they want to marry you. Or you will hear because I love you. Then you must think about how you feel when you are in their presence. People sometimes confuse love with profoundly caring. Love is a word that must be displayed, demonstrated, viewed, acted, and exhibited. Merely stating that I love you with not a demonstration or display is a statement with no facts. Why you are marrying someone just because you love them. It is way more than that because love can fade or change like the seasons. God prepared Adam to receive Eve. God put Adan in a deep sleep and removes something of value from him to give to Eve. Marriage is more than words; it is life.

Before I Do, Let Us Talk About - Cheating

This is a subject that has many outcomes. Everyone's definition of cheat is not the same. For instance, if I do not love you or say I love you, it is okay to cheat on you. Because in their mind, it is not cheating. To have this conversation, you must understand the definition of cheating as it relates to a relationship. The act of cheating carries these actions: Deceitful, false, devious, wrong, deception, selfish, fraud, tricking and bamboozling.

Ask your partner what they consider cheating. People do not consider flirting cheating; that precisely what it is. My definition of cheat is: when you are in a relationship, and you become unfaithful to the other person by sexual, flirting, emotional, and physical all that is CHEATING. Conversation plays a big part in creating an environment to become unfaithful. The Bible says, keep your conversation yea or no. This is a rule to go by. If you don't say it to dad or mom, don't say it to another man or woman that is not your spouse.

Before I Do, Let Us Talk About - Drugs and Alcohol

This is a conversation that must be talked about way before I do. Often in a relationship, people hide this issue. Most of the time, partners have. No idea that their partner is abusing drugs until it is too late. If you love your partner, be honest and let them know you have a habit that can damage their marriage. Any drug use can cause a marriage to go sour. There is no small level of drug use. Some will say I need it because of my medical condition. Then allow that person to speak with your doctor to see if there is anything else that he/she can prescribe that will give the same results.

Before I Do, Let Us Talk About - Jealous

Jealousy is fear base and can damage a relationship and marriage. Questions to ask your partner: What makes you jealous? How do you act when you are jealous? What level of jealousy can you control? When a partner becomes extremely jealous, it will destroy relationships and marriages. I believe four ingredients make up jealousy: fear, insecurity, pride, and pain.

Let talk about the aspects of fear when it comes to jealousy. When you fear someone else is taking your position in their life. You panic and become frightened or alarmed that you are being replaced. In reality, you have not been replaced. But insecurity tells you that you have many unmet needs or promises that you did not keep in the relationship. Now you are fearful that someone else will get the affection and love you now have.

Insecurity joins in when you have been unstable in the relationship. You have made promises you did not keep, and your actions were doubtful. Listen, if you do not honor your own words, why do you expect the other person? In a marriage, your words must be true at all times.

Promises must be fulfilled, and actions must be justified. Simply stated, do what you say and say what you are doing. You cannot make a promise, and when it's time to deliver, you change your mind. This type of action will undoubtedly bring doubt into your relationship. The way to solve this is to not make a promise you cannot fulfill. Please do not say I will try.

Each time you give your words and do not honor them, which leaves room for your reputation to be tarnished.

Insecurity brings much sorrow to your relationship. Holding it inside makes things worse. There is a way to talk about a situation without getting angry. Remember, your partner did not cause your fear, insecurity, pride, or pain. It is all self-afflicted.

Pain is when you are not comfortable because of an injury to your pride. In a relationship, there will be times when your pride will suffer pain. But you understand that is self-worth in your own dignity. An injury to your pride is very discomforting and miserable, which causes irritation and unstable emotions. Pain is something that we must endure in life, but constant pain becomes long-suffering. Often when your pride is hurt, you see things only one way, which is your way. In a relationship, you must humble yourself to exhort your marriage. You cannot expect someone to marry you when your pride has told you you're better than your partner.

You may talk down to them, unaware of it. But not change either. Remember to change your lifestyle, and then the mind will change as well. Also, know that the emotional pain of jealousy walks hand in hand with pride. Then here comes the pain, which causes you to exhibit anger, and rage, which is unrestrained anger violent.

Before I Do, Let Us Talk About - Going to Church Together

How often will we go to church together? You must express how important the church is to you. How important to attend the same church? If you marry a pastor, it is understood that you would support his vision. If neither of you are pastors, then you must decide on a church to attend. Going to church together brings unity, strength, wholeness, and harmony in the marriage. If he/she has a ministry, decide if you will support the ministry. Don't act as if you are supporting it while dating and then getting married and stopping all support. Also, don't take over their ministry; you are a team, and each of you is important, but only one person is the head of the ministry. The other one supports.

Now, women, your first obligation is to the Lord, the second is to your own husband; don't get it twisted. Also, to be on one accord, you must walk in the same directions. Men, your first love is to God; the second is to your wife. Your church belongs to God.

Before I Do, Let Us Talk About – Childhood Trauma

Discussing this issue before marriage is well needed. This is a conversation that must occur, and it is important to know about your spouse's childhood life. Often most people cover up the hurt from childhood because it is so painful. Fear, shame, embarrassment and sadness all are housed in the heart of an unspoken toxin childhood. They rather ignore it or pretend nothing ever happened at all. Also, these issues are not discussed before marriage because no one wants to be judged because they love their parents. Childhood pain waits to see a repeated pattern to surface in the current relationship. Painful emotional wounds can channel into adulthood which will bring back inner hurt and pain.

Once discussed, you will have the opportunity to understand the wounds, pains and disappointments. Do not begin to pass judgment to the point that you will say. "that's why he/she is like that" When listening, keep in mind, it is like peeling an onion; each layer will bring tears. When the pain is hard to bear or hear, it is okay to step back and take a break before continuing the process. Remember to listen with an open heart and an active ear to hear without apathy (boredom) but empathy (compassion).

You may start off by asking about their childhood and ask what you liked about it. What did you not like?

Before I Do, Let Us Talk About – Disagreements

There will be disagreements in a relationship; in a family in a marriage, we are all created uniquely. Our thoughts are different, and our point views of how we see things are as well. When you disagree, there is no right or wrong, simply misdirected or misguided. Even when one spouse is misguided, permit him or her to re-claim their self-respect and their trust in you. Do not continue to have them relive the feeling of hurt for being misguided and not in tune with what actually happens.

Establishing rules ahead for any disagreements and a safe place for either person to go to cool down; when they are upset. For example, in school, a child gets upset and starts screaming, yelling, throwing things. There is a place in the classroom that is called "time out." When that child enters that spot, they are there to cool off. The teachers do not bother them until they have gone from a 10 to a 1. Only the child knows when they have calmed down. You must set up a place that you both agree is the time-out spot. This spot is for the spouse to calm down before trying to continue the disagreement. Some people exercise where they transfer that energy into a positive setting.

You may walk away, listen to music because it enters the body without your permission and will change your mood.

Also, agree there is no winner or loser; you both had the opportunity to voice your opinion positively. As children, our parents would dispute before whichever one benefits both persons that should be agreed upon. When you say I was right, the other person was wrong, and in a marriage, if they are wrong, you both are wrong. In other words, there is no loser or winner, only a mutual understanding. If one spouse keeps says I won, the other spouse loses and develops bitterness and offenses.

To attack disagreement at the root, make sure you are in touch with your own feelings and conquer your issues. It is hard to have a marriage when the relationship has been damaged by resentment and dislike. You both would have lost because the marriage relationship is damaged.

Notes:

Notes:

Notes:

Notes:

Notes:

Notes:

Notes:

____

____

____

____

____

____

____

____

____

____

____

____

____

____

____

____

____

____

____

____

Other books by this Author

21 Days of Throne Room Prayers

21 Days of Prayer and Fasting

Interceding for your family

What is Marriage? Marriage is What?

Will You Marry Me?

Finding God's Divine Purpose for Your Life

About the Author

Dr. Mary Lewallen is the second child of nine children. She is married to Bishop Ken Lewallen, who has co-labored with her in ministry. Their mandate is to strengthen couples, marriages, individuals, and families through godly training, penmanship, and the Holy Spirit's leading. Couples wishing they sought further directions before they said I do. There are hurting marriages because neither he/she understands what is behind the dos of a marriage. Couples will continue to work in the church and their jobs where they are victorious and go home to defeat. This book helps you understand the before and after jitters when you say, "I do." The word "do" means fix something, prepare something, organize something, or work out something. With that said, each person who says "I do" agrees to prepare beforehand, fix what is broken, and work out what is wrong. Marriage has its extraordinary challenges, problems, disagreements, and points of view.

Dr. Lewallen understands marriage through the leading of the Holy Spirit. This book can be used as a tool to help you in your marriage. Therefore, when you say, I do, note that your actions may say, I DON'T.

Thank You for Reading

Thank you for dedicating some of your time to read my book. I hope you are enjoying and believe by faith that God will answer your prayers. I know some of you might not understand why you brought this book, but God does. If your prayers are responded to, and you will spare the time to write a sentence or two about what God did as a testimony, please do. Also, what are your thoughts about this book?

I will love to hear from you. If you would like me to put you on my prayer list, please email me your name and email address, and I will begin with a prayer for you by name. If you would like a signed copy of this book, please attend one of my prayer events. I encourage you to post it.

You may contact me through email:

Throneroomprayerss@gmail.com

Praying Always,

Dr. Mary Lewallen

93

Dr. Mary Lewallen

94

95

97